Surviving the Garden of Eatin'

Surprising Biblical Insights to Enjoy Optimal Wellness

Michele Neil-Sherwood, DO & Mark Sherwood, ND
www.Sherwood.TV

Unless otherwise noted, scripture taken from the Holy Bible, English Standard Version Copyright © 2001 by Crossway

Cover design *www.MikeLoomis.CO*

Cartoons by Eric Lee and Mike Loomis

An important note to the reader:

This book is not intended as a substitute for the medical advice of physicians. Readers should regularly consult a physician in matters relating to health and particularly with respect to any symptoms that may require diagnosis or medical attention. Do not make changes to your diet, exercise, or intake of prescription medications without consulting your physician.

The names of patients and other details in the stories have been changed to protect the privacy of our patients.

www.fmidr.com

This book is dedicated to all of our wonderful patients around the world who have inspired us, as well as our family, friends, and staff who support us as we all carry the torch for true wellness.

Mark and Michele
www.fmidr.com
www.Sherwood.TV

Contents

Introduction

Why We Wrote this for You

We've spoken about health and wellness on six continents. We're passionate about the subject because we care about people, and we're saddened by how many people suffer needlessly.

As we've traveled, often to bring medical care and insight to impoverished areas of the world, we've seen something alarming—and surprising.

One of the biggest health challenges people face around the world is the "American diet." As fast food and fake food spread, so do sickness and disease. The medical community in third-world countries are increasingly afraid of what the Western world is exporting.

Christians across the globe pray diligently for health. But, barring a miracle, nothing overrides the damaging effects of the standard American diet.

We understand. Food is a temptation. Just as it was in the Garden of Eden. And food is still a temptation in our garden of eatin' (That is the new type of garden we have created where everything is about food). But listen carefully: the consequences of dining regularly in the garden of eatin' can be dire.

Mark's Story

I (Mark) was a frumpy, and sometimes chunky, kid. As a relative weakling, classmates often picked on me. Even today, when I look in the mirror, I see that dumpy, frumpy child.

Fast forward a few decades. After trying for a couple of years (and failing) to make it in professional baseball, I became a police officer. While working there, I began to observe a very concerning pattern. I watched how men and women would join the department in the best shape of their lives—and die in the worst shape of their lives shortly after retirement. And they weren't living very long in age. The life expectancy of a retired male police officer was sixty-six years old. This fact shocked me, because I was on track to be one of the people who made this average life span so low. During my time in this career, I saw people die, I observed the chaotic potential of society, and I looked into the eyes of evil.

One day, it hit me like a ton of bricks. What we're doing, and how we're living, isn't working. In fact, it's killing us. This had affected my family as well as the men and women with whom I was serving. What was going on? This began my tireless pursuit for answers. I was committed to understand what really makes us thrive— and what drives both good and bad decisions, with resulting positive or negative consequences.

Using the same insights we outline in this book, I took hold of my health and decided to make it a life mission to help others.

Michele's story

I (Michele) grew up feeling like I was a parent to my parents. This statement isn't meant to imply that my adoptive parents didn't love me, or to make them appear like bad people. My father suffered a tragic accident and was disabled when I was twelve years old. A physical accident sometimes hinders more than just the physical aspect of a person. The emotional and spiritual state of a human being can be injured by physical injury.

He later became riddled with disease and, as time passed, became morbidly obese. Later, my mother became progressively disabled after she retired. With their health issues, I found myself trying to rescue them, and help remedy the situation any way I could.

Through the years, I saw them both try, and fail, to get their health under control. They tried every fad diet without success. I watched them try numerous vitamin pill regimens and read health magazines and books, all to no avail. It grieved me that they couldn't make lasting progress.

As a result, I took on a "compulsive health nut" approach. I loved my parents but was horrified at the sickness, disease, and obesity issues that afflicted their lives. I felt compelled to help them find a better way.

I read all kinds of health magazines and found myself delving into exercise. I climbed the ranks of judo and quickly achieved a brown belt.

My high school years were extremely difficult, as I worked three jobs to help support my family. I worked so much that I almost flunked out of high school and was even labeled dyslexic. I found a new martial art, Tae Kwon Do. I climbed the ranks quickly and in eleven months received my black belt. I set my eyes on the Olympics, with a dream to be an Olympian when Tae Kwon Do had its debut as a spectator sport.

After graduating high school, a knee injury brought my dreams of Olympic glory to an abrupt end. So I pursued massage therapy. Because of a lack of finances, I was forced to live in my car for several months until I built up enough paying massage clients to afford an apartment. By the early 1990s, I was earning just enough money to rent an apartment. For the first six months, I had no furniture and lived by candlelight to save on utility bills.

My massage therapy career took me on many rewarding journeys to study with some of the greatest health experts. I finished a degree in naturopathic medicine in 1995. Then, after a massage client encouraged me to pursue my passion for health, I enrolled in medical school.

I believed that medical school was the key to truly help people get well. I not only wanted to be in the best health *personally*, but I wanted that for every one of my patients.

It's worth the effort

As you can see, we both had plenty of opportunities to quit. Our drive is fueled from our past experiences of overcoming, and from helping our patients overcome. We won't quit, and we want you to be infected with that attitude as well.

Our society has more knowledge regarding personal well-being than ever before, yet we're unhealthier than ever before. The numbers of people afflicted with inflammation, weight issues, metabolic syndrome, and diabetes is rising. If we have all this information at our disposal, what's the disconnect?

Information isn't the answer to health. And medicine isn't the answer to getting well. Diets don't work. Over-exercising doesn't work, and you can't out-supplement an unhealthy lifestyle.

Even God will not override the consequences of our repeatedly poor choices. An example of this would be continuing to break traffic laws, receive repeated citations, and always expect God to pay the fine. This would be a misuse of the concept of grace.

But there is abundant grace available to you today. There is a path to wellness. As you begin this journey, remember you're not alone.

Every tree in the garden was good for food...
Except one.

Chapter 1

You Were Made for Health

We all believe something.

Whether it's faith in God, in people, or in science—our beliefs shape our choices and our lifestyle.

When it comes to your health, what do you believe?

We ask because what you believe is the foundation of your life. Our foundation is the Word of God, and it's the source of much of our belief about health. Whether you share our faith or not, you'll be amazed at how helpful the Bible is when it comes to your health, your hope, and your life.

Wouldn't it be wonderful to believe that you were actually made to enjoy health? You were. This was God's original intent for us.

In the garden

Let's go back to the garden. Not the Olive Garden restaurant, the Garden of Eden. Although I'm pretty sure olives grew there, and they did have endless salad (and no "dressing").

In the beginning, there was health.

And God said, "Behold, I have given you *every plant yielding seed* that is on the face of all the earth, and *every tree with seed in its fruit.* You shall have them for food."... And God saw everything that he had made, and behold, *it was very good.*

(Genesis 1:29, 31 emphasis added)

Life was pretty simple for Adam and Eve. Take care of the garden, love each other, eat from the wondrous array of fruits and vegetables, and live forever. There was no sickness or disease—or even death. Until the original power couple decided to eat from the forbidden *cupcake* tree. (You don't really think it was an *apple* tree, do you?)

This theme of goodness, health, and peace continues through the Bible, into the New Testament. Scripture goes a little bit deeper, looking at the book of 3rd John, verse 2.

"Beloved, I pray that all may go well with you and that you may be in good health, as it goes well with your soul."

Most people understand that God is all about *spiritual* health. Some realize that God is also concerned with our *emotional* health. But we somehow see a disconnect in society in regard to God's design for *physical* health.

Lack of physical health is not our Creator's plan; often it's a sign of spiritual brokenness. For example, when people live in chronic fear or stress, medical experts agree this has a harmful effect on the body.

What about chronic sadness or shame? We all know about "comfort food," which means we acknowledge there is much need for comfort in this world. But (and we all know this deep down) the answer to our pain is not on the tree of cupcakes.

We have the answer, because we are loved, and designed for health—in all areas of our being. It was—and still is—God's intention.

And the garden of earth, despite its fall, still produces pretty amazing food. The food your body and soul have been hungry for.

Have we also lost our identity?

Your driver's license, or other official document, is tied to your identity. Your identification reveals your name, where you live, when you were born, current citizenship, and more.

Adam and Eve lost their identity—all because of a doughnut or some kind of fruit. But before that fall, they *forgot* their identity.

It's easy for us to forget who we are and what we were created for. Knowing who you are is the best way to combat temptation and make heathy choices in every area of life.

11

For example, if someone offers a cigarette to a smoker, they might say, "No thank you, I'm trying to quit." But let's look at this situation in the light of *identity*.

The response reinforces an identity of someone who is still addicted to tobacco but is "trying" to change a behavior—as opposed to someone who views themself as healthy and not interested in cigarettes. See the difference? The same applies to food temptations.

Self-control is one of the fruits of spirit and is part of who we are as believers. We can remember our identity and ask God to help us. You are not a citizen of this world, and captive to its bad habits and dysfunctions. You are a citizen of heaven and an ambassador for the Kingdom of God. As an ambassador, you can bring those beliefs, mindsets, and practices to this world.

Remembering our citizenship

If we are citizens of a healthy place (and we are), the question then becomes, "What would a healthy person eat?"

And, "What would a person, who loved themself in the way God intends, eat?"

They would put food in their body that expressed love. They would treat their bodies and minds like temples—because we are God's temple on earth.

Adam and Eve lost sight of their identity, and they forgot that they were given guidelines based on *love*.

We can approach food choices based on love because we are loved by a God and Savior who wants us to be healthy. When Jesus walked the earth, he represented God's love and purpose. He fed and healed people.

Sadly, most people who are "trying" to be healthy are limiting themselves to their own willpower. And most fail. But if we'll stay connected to the truth that God wants us to enjoy health and long life—and that He wants to *help* us on the journey—we'll find power beyond our weaknesses.

The Roots

As we imagine the Garden of Eden, let's examine the root causes of sickness, disease, and death—so we don't fall into the same trap.

There are six possible reasons you've failed to improve your health—and sabotaged your goals with bad choices. And they're all FRAUDS, which is an acronym for:

F = Fear
R = Resentment
A = Anger
U = Unforgiveness
D = Disappointment
S = Shame

Let's take a look at each of these.

Fear

After Adam said, "I heard the sound of you in the garden, and I was afraid, because I was naked, and I hid myself." Fear pulled Adam away from God (and Eve). But this wasn't the first time he (and Eve) chose to listen to fear.

A few hours earlier, they believed a lie, and fear arose. They feared missing out on what they *thought* God was keeping from them. Instead of believing, they questioned.

Sure, fear can keep you out of trouble. Before you pull out from a traffic light, you look left and right, based on a healthy fear of harm. But fear can also keep you *in* trouble.

When I, (Mark) was growing up I struggled with approval. I still do, to some extent. The fear of rejection stems back to childhood—being an only child, adopted, and not one of the cool guys in school.

If you know there is something new you need to do, you know there will be fear. You have to do it afraid. Growth happens when you step outside of your comfort zone, and it will require action.

Resentment

Have you ever had the experience of seeing someone you know and wanting to walk the other way? That's resentment.

I (Michele) look back on the hurts I experienced in my younger years—wounds of abandonment, abusive relationships, personal injury, and homelessness. Little did I realize resentment is like an infection that won't heal. Eventually the wound of resentment turns into anger.

Anger

Anger will drive our blood pressure up, which can drive up our cortisol. Cortisol drives blood sugar, and when blood sugar goes up, it drives insulin. When insulin is up in a chronic way, you'll begin to store fat and eventually end up with the syndrome of insulin resistance and the onset of chronic disease.

See how emotion can easily impact our health?

In the early spring of last year, a young man came to see us for help with his weight. He had tried every diet and weight-loss strategy—and even tried a few types of diet pills. He turned to us as his last hope. In order to get to the root, we like to ask a lot of questions. After all, we want success.

We asked, "How long have you struggled with weight?"

"Since childhood."

"Did your parents show any favoritism toward you or your sibling?"

"Yes, my brother was their favorite."

"Did your brother struggle with weight?"

"No," he snapped. We could see emotions rising up.

15

So we asked, "How did they handle that with you?"

"Well, my parents used to tell me to lose weight—and be more like my brother."

We could feel the burden he carried, even though his parents had long since passed. He went on to marry a woman who seemed to be able to eat anything she wanted and not gain weight. When she told him he needed to lose weight, all the fear, resentment, and anger came rushing back like a bad dream. These were the roots of his food addiction.

Sometimes we have to go back to our childhood years to find the root of anger, or any one of the FRAUDS for that matter.

Unforgiveness

God doesn't expect you to be perfect. We sure aren't. But what we expect, and what you should expect, is perfect effort. This means when you fall down, there are three choices. Number one, you can lie there and let resentment turn to anger. Number two, you can cry and stay in the sadness and wallow in the pain. But there's a third option.

You can dust yourself off and say, "Well, I fell. It happens sometimes when you move. So I choose to forgive myself. And I choose to get up."

When it comes to forgiveness, why not begin with you? Are you willing to forgive yourself? (God is always willing.)

Disappointment

The long-term effects of fear, resentment, anger, and unforgiveness create an outlook of continual disappointment and despair.

We prescribe a unique tool to every one of our patients: healing words. We recommend replacements for statements like, "I'm a victim of my father's alcoholism," "I'm fat and ugly," or, "I'll never lose weight." Instead, create and speak positive statements about you and your future, along with scriptures that build faith.

Pay attention to your words, and prescribe healthful words instead. If you don't take disappointment seriously and treat it like a deadly disease, you may fall victim to the final of the FRAUDS.

Shame

We are often ashamed of our actions, and even ashamed of life's twists and turns that were out of our control. Instead of seeing ourselves as a person who's overcoming, we see someone who's been overcome.

People who hide shame often over-talk and make fun of themselves. They're always hiding—which is easy to do on social media. The problem is, social media is a breeding ground for comparison and shame.

Altogether, FRAUDS lie about who you truly are. Don't let those lies tempt you to hide from God like Adam and Eve did.

17

Are you hiding?

In Genesis 3:8, after Adam and Eve ate the forbidden buffet, they felt ashamed and hid from God.

When we fall for temptation, eat whatever is clearly out of bounds, we often do exactly what they did—hide from God. Why would we be ashamed to connect with the One Who loves us so much He gave His Son to save us? Why would we hide from the only one who can strengthen and guide us from the inside out?

There is no fear in love. And God is love.

If you're serious about the journey to wellness, let's get rid of the self-sabotage that's rooted in fear and shame. God loves you and wants to help you. Period.

Don't own your ailments

Another way people hide from health is by owning their ailments. This doesn't mean we should not take a diagnosis or medical recommendation seriously; it simply means we don't adopt a disease as part of ourselves.

We actually believe that diseases may not even exist! Before you decide we have lost our minds, let us explain. Diseases are nothing more than groups of symptoms clustered together. They are then named "disease names." If you are able to eliminate the symptoms, the "names" can go away. So, let's not *only* seek to find the correct disease; rather, let's seek to find the root of the symptoms and bring correction.

Have you ever heard anyone say, *"My* diabetes has got the best of me today"? Or *"My* high blood pressure"?

You're a citizen of healthy heaven. Did God give those challenges to one of his citizens? Really? Think about that long and hard.

God's intention and hope for you is health—spirit, soul, and body. This includes peace of mind, freedom from fear and shame.

When you seek you will find

A few months ago, a woman walked into our clinic. She had an earlier visit at a hospital down the street, and was headed to a counseling appointment with a dietician about diet her recent diagnosis of Type 2 diabetes.

As she entered the counseling office, something didn't feel right to her. She was told she would be on medication forever and would never be free from diabetes. So she left the building, walked down the sidewalk, and ended up in our clinic.

We believe God directed her to us. She walked to our front desk and asked our receptionist about the clinic. At the same time, I (Mark) happened to walk by.

I looked her in the eyes and said, "God sent you here, and we're gonna help you. You're *not* a diabetic. I won't hear those words spoken in your presence ever again. Do what we tell you, and you'll be free from that nonsense."

And she did. Four months later, after taking steps to choose health, her tests confirmed she was no longer diabetic. She no longer needed to take insulin. With proper attention to lifestyle and its components of nutrition, rest, and stress management, her disease went into remission.

She was in a system that was trying to *manage* her disease, and she walked into another system. A kingdom system is a system that teaches the components of health, and giving the body what it needs to heal and stay well. The world system wants to manage. The kingdom system wants to heal.

When failure can be your friend

Most people in the Western world have tried many fad diets, quick fixes, and even weight-loss pills. Most have failed and ended up right back where they started—or even worse off.

What's responsible for this failure? We know what to do, and often know how to do it, but can't seem to stay the course. (Sounds like Adam and Eve in the Garden, right?)

Instead of continuing to "try" harder, why not ask God to show us the root of the problem?

Digest and Decide

What seems clear to me from this chapter:

_____

_____

_____

_____

_____

One choice or small step I'm willing to make right now:

_____

_____

_____

_____

"May I suggest the colon cleanse for dessert?"

Chapter 2

The Fall of Health

A certain administrator from a well-known cancer hospital came to see us one day. She was here as a patient, and we were discussing her food choices, and particularly the food options available at her hospital.

We were shocked. We assumed this facility served organic food, fresh vegetables, and other items that promoted healing.

"Oh, no, we don't do that anymore. We went to the regular old standard hospital menu items," she said with disappointment. They switched because the staff and patients complained. The more she learned from being a patient at our clinic, the more she saw that the hospital was serving poison to cancer patients.

We actually heard stories about seriously ill patients being served soft drinks and doughnuts to celebrate milestones in their recovery.

Long story short, with our help, the hospital changed their menu in a few months. If we find this sort of unhealthy food promoted in hospitals, how diligent must we be in our everyday choices? Reading labels before you put things in the grocery buggy is a good start to any wellness journey. Most items found on the ingredient list can't be pronounced, let alone understood.

It's a jungle out there

In *The Wizard of Oz*, Dorothy famously said, "I don't think we're in Kansas anymore."

In the context of this book, I'd put it this way: "We're not in the Garden anymore." No, we are now living in the garden of eatin', and it is eating us alive.

The topic of health—specifically, healthful food—is probably the biggest area of deception on planet Earth. Don't believe me? Have you ever considered that the first story of deception in the Bible centered around what to eat and what *not* to eat?

One result—then, and to this day—is needless suffering.

People worry about their health, then knowingly eat and drink foods that degrade their health. Churches promote gatherings with pizza, doughnuts, cookies, and cola—and actually contribute to the poor eating habits and unhealthiness of their congregations. With all the tools and technologies we have to save lives (medications, procedures, doctors), *preventable* diseases are still ending lives at alarming rates.

Why try to pray something away that you can change with a simple trip to the grocery store?

Look at the disease of cancer. The same number of people are dying from cancers now as they were forty years ago. Why are we losing so many people to something we proclaimed "war" on in 1975? As a society, we are losing the war on cancer, and we're losing badly.

As an anecdote, when we visit people in the hospital, we're astounded to see them served food that's been proven to cause the very same disease they're in the hospital for.

These disease trends tell us a big story, so let's get a bit more specific. Someone dies every thirty-four seconds from heart disease. Every forty seconds, an American has a heart attack. In America, 2,200 people die from heart disease each day. And 610,000 Americans die of heart disease every single year.

In the time it took to read the paragraph above, four people died from heart disease. Wouldn't it be wonderful to prevent those four deaths?

Trouble in the temple

Jesus, in his last week of life on earth, went into the temple—the place of worship in those days. But instead of prayers, He saw money-changers and those selling "fast-food" animal offerings.

The scene broke his heart.

With a whip he braided himself, He started flipping tables, driving people out, and shouting.

> "'My house shall be called a house of
> prayer,' but you make it a den of robbers."
> (Matthew 21:13)

27

Many refer to this story as "the cleansing of the temple." But that's not the end of the story; it's just the beginning.

In the next verses, Jesus healed blind and lame people. He drove evil out of the temple so people could be healed in the temple.

Our bodies are the place where the Holy Spirit lives.

> "Or do you not know that your body
> is a temple of the Holy Spirit within you,
> whom you have from God? You are not your
> own, for you were bought with a price. So
> glorify God in your body."
> (1 Corinthians 6:19–20)

Jesus' presence in the ancient temple is related to His presence inside our physical bodies. Our bodies are designed to be places of healing. God made our bodies to heal themselves in a miraculous, organized, physiological way.

The corrupt people whom Jesus drove out of the temple had stopped protecting the sacred place.

But we can guard our bodies and minds from the poison of the world. A lot of corruption has been allowed to enter our body, either by choice (food, cosmetics, drinks) or by environmental exposure from our toxic atmosphere. Because we have the mind of Christ, let's do our best to drive it all out—by equipping our body, mind, and spirit to be whole.

God also created a wondrous system to remove harmful foods—it's called the detox system. Our bodies are designed to represent healing in its totality.

Are we living longer?

Perhaps we're not living longer. We're simply *dying* longer.

Think about this concept: maybe Satan does not want to end your physical life at all. Maybe he wants to extend your life, keep you sicker longer, and make you hate living. Maybe his plan is really about using a "sick you" as long as possible to negatively influence others. Maybe he wants people to believe sickness is a part of living and therefore, people are actually suffering in a death process for more years.

In our country, the process of the end-of-life is being extended, but the quality of life is not being extended.

One in three children today are predicted to be Type 2 diabetic by the time they're forty. This type of diabetes is preventable and reversible; it should not exist.

Probably the most shocking statistic is about autism. Forty years ago, it was one in forty-thousand. Today, it's one in forty. By the year 2050, some predictions indicate it's going to be one in two Americans.

We can bounce along in denial, hide in shame, or face the failure.

The designer of life

We might not be in the Garden anymore, but the Gardener is still with us.

When we consider the creator of the universe—the creator of *you*—we must not look to modern society, the state of our health, rampant disasters, sickness, disease, and suffering. Watch the television news, and you'll see we've drifted and crashed a long way from the garden of health and peace.

The point is, if you want to believe that God's plan for you is health, you need to know something about God's heart.

We can see His heart reflected in original creation. God is all about giving hope, producing life, generating love, and providing immeasurable spiritual food for growth.

First, let's look at hope. Hope gives us something to look forward to. Hope provides the reason and motivation to press onward. God always gives us hope because He is good.

Second, let's examine life. What is life, anyway? It is more, much more, than physical life. However, God does want us to have a joyous and fruitful physical life. He provides this in our amazing temple (our body), which He created specifically for His Spirit to reside in.

Third, there is love. What a word and what a concept! God gives love and *is* love. God's love has no end. Even when we don't love, he showers us with love. As

Romans 5:8 establishes, "While we were yet sinners, Christ (God's son) died for us." That is pretty amazing love.

Fourth, let's dive into spiritual food. With the proper food, we will properly grow. God's heart is full of plenty of spiritual food because it contains His Word. His Word (the Bible) provides all the spiritual nutrition we will ever need. But we must choose to use what is readily available.

How can our heart trust our Creator and become more like His heart?

1. **Daily realize God is hope.** Eternal hope cannot be put on a person, career, or money. It needs to be placed squarely upon God.

2. **Understand that the life you lead is not your own.** God made you. You are not an accident or result of a big bang in the cosmos. He made the very concept of life. Therefore, in Him is life.

3. **Allow God to love you.** If you allow it, it will happen. He loves you no matter what, but if you trust in His love, your experience will be undeniable.

4. **Trust in God's spiritual food to grow.** Read His Word through the Bible. Listen for His Word through people, circumstances, and the whispers of Holy Spirit. By hearing, believing, and acting upon His Word, you will grow.

5. **Be thankful on purpose.** When we look, we'll find an endless list of things to be grateful for.

31

Thank God for your health, home, family, spouse, friends, clothes, food, and hope.

6. **Be honest with God.** Don't hold back. Share your deepest thoughts with Him. Why hold in negative thoughts and feelings? He can be trusted and only wants the best for you.

All these are basic ingredients for a life of peace and health.

Digest and Decide

What seems clear to me from this chapter:

_____

_____

_____

_____

_____

One choice I'm willing to make right now:

_____

_____

_____

_____

_____

"I'm here because of **your** side effects."
"Are you kidding me? I wouldn't be here
without **your** side effects!"

Chapter 3

The Enemy

When you consider humanity's ever-increasing struggle—and stated desire—for wellness, is there any doubt that we're in a battle? Shouldn't we be further along?

Just look at the upward trend in the use of pharmaceutical medications. We are not against pharmaceutical drugs, but we are very passionately against the overuse and unnecessary use of medications.

Why? Because medications are not about *healing* disease. Medications are about *managing* conditions.

If we believe 3rd John 2 that God is all about healing, then we can't believe God is completely satisfied by the mere management of conditions. Let's look at Galatians 5:19–20:

> "Now the works of the flesh are evident: sexual immorality, impurity, sensuality, idolatry, *sorcery*, enmity, strife, jealousy, fits of anger, rivalries, dissensions, divisions."
>
> (Emphasis added)

The Apostle Paul, under what we believe to be God's direction, is talking to the Galatian church about the decline of their lifestyle. Regarding the word *sorcery*, the original Greek word is *pharmakeia*. This is the same word by which we derive *pharmacy* and *pharmaceuticals*.

There seems to be symbiotic view of pharmakeia and sorcery working hand in hand. This seems to indicate that a dependence upon drugs to bring about healing is a form of substitution—or distraction from the real source of health. A sole dependence upon drugs to heal certainly doesn't agree with the biblical principle, does it?

Insuring health

There seems to be no escaping many forms of insurance in our society. Homeowners, auto, health, and endless other forms of coverage.

The question to consider is this: When does insurance pay?

The answer is: When something goes wrong.

When does car insurance pay? When the car breaks. Does car insurance pay for putting air in your tires? Does it pay for oil changes? Tune ups? Fuel? No.

When does health insurance pay? When you're sick.

"Health insurance" is probably the improper term for that particular protective mechanism. It's not *health* insurance, it's *sick* insurance. It's catastrophe insurance.

When something breaks or goes wrong in our bodies, we're sadly mistaken if we believe health insurance will pay for our "tune ups" and "fuel." Health insurance is important, but too many people have been lulled into dependence on pharmaceutical and insurance companies. (And in our view, more money is spent on the advertising a medication—to fuel this dependence—than is invested in the research and development of the product.)

How many people's insurance premiums and deductibles go up every year? We believe that if we pay our $5,000 deductible, the insurance company will pay for everything. But we forgot they took an additional five thousand more dollars from us over and above our monthly premium. Do not be deceived by this tactic. Insurance is a for-profit business, and consistent customers are the best source of consistent insurance income. Aiming to get people well would bankrupt big business.

We need to understand how to keep that money in our pockets.

That's what "well care" does—it keeps the deductible in your pocket. Every year.

An ounce of Prevention

You've heard the old adage, "An ounce of prevention is worth a pound of cure." The same applies to insurance, maintenance, and fuel for our health.

The problem, and the concept of prevention, was actually initiated in the Garden of Eden.

"Then God said let us make man in our image according to our likeness. Let them have dominion over the fish of the sea, over the birds of the air, and over the cattle, *over all the earth* and over every creeping thing that creeps on earth"

(Genesis 1:26, emphasis added)

In the context of the topic of food and God's provision for humankind, the word *earth* is synonymous with *dirt*. This means we were intended to have dominion or control over the dirt, which is where our food comes from.

"And God said, 'See I have given you every herb that yields seed which is on the face of all the earth and every tree whose fruit yields seeds *to you it shall be for food*'"

(Genesis 1:29, emphasis added)

We see clearly that plants were created to be our food. Makes you wonder what God thinks about statements like, "I hate vegetables." God made these plants to provide nourishment, and even gave us herbs and seasonings to make meals taste amazing. Plants, in their original form and not genetically modified, and are designed to be our food. In fresh and raw food, you find not only the macronutrients, you find the micronutrients and enzymes. All of the important components of healing are found in natures fruits and vegetables.

40

"And out of the ground the Lord made every tree grow that is pleasant to the sight and good for food. The Tree of Life was also in the midst of the garden and the tree of knowledge of good and evil"
(Genesis 2:9)

All this creation of food occurred before God made any animals or created Adam and Eve. Do you think they hated vegetables? Of course not. Before you put any food *in* your mouth, try expressing these words *out* of your mouth: "I love vegetables. They are made for my good. They are fuel for my healthy body!"

Digging the dirt

"And the Lord God formed man of the dust of the ground and breathed into his nostrils the breath of life, and man became a living being"
(Genesis 2:7)

In Genesis 1:26, God gave humankind authority over the *earth,* right? If Adam was formed from the dirt (the earth), humankind also has authority over the "earth" of our physical bodies. We are made from dirt, but we have authority over the dirt.

But as often happens with authority, there are attacks.

The enemy of God is also the enemy of every human being. Adam and Eve were totally in alignment in their relationship with God and each other. Perfect peace.

"Now the serpent was more crafty than any other beast of the field that the Lord God had made. He said to the woman, 'Did God actually say, 'You[a] shall not eat of any tree in the garden'?'

And the woman said to the serpent, 'We may eat of the fruit of the trees in the garden, but God said, 'You shall not eat of the fruit of the tree that is in the midst of the garden, neither shall you touch it, lest you die.'"

But the serpent said to the woman, 'You will not surely die. For God knows that when you eat of it your eyes will be opened, and you will be like God, knowing good and evil.'

So when the woman saw that the tree was good for food, and that it was a delight to the eyes, and that the tree was to be desired to make one wise, she took of its fruit and ate, and she also gave some to her husband who was with her, and he ate.

Then the eyes of both were opened, and they knew that they were naked. And they sewed fig leaves together and made themselves loincloths.

Do you see the dramatic change in self-awareness? Before they ate of the forbidden tree, they were not aware of the flesh. Oh, that we could walk with less awareness of the flesh!

> And they heard the sound of the Lord God walking in the garden in the cool of the day, and the man and his wife hid themselves from the presence of the Lord God among the trees of the garden.
>
> But the Lord God called to the man and said to him, 'Where are you?' And he said, 'I heard the sound of you in the garden, and I was afraid, because I was naked, and I hid myself.'"
>
> (Genesis 3:1–10)

If it weren't so tragic, I'd find it funny that God would ask, "Where are you?" as if God didn't know where they were. Some Bible scholars translate that question to be "*Why* are you where you are?" That's the real question.

So we must understand a couple important points. Satan, the enemy, is all about deception and substitution—as we discussed earlier with the concept of sorcery or pharmakeia. We're always tempted with counterfeits of the real thing. Counterfeit truth, fake foods, and shallow relationships.

But we have free will and must choose rightly—for ourselves and for our loved ones. Adam could have—and should have—intervened before Eve ate the forbidden cupcake, and certainly should not have taken a bite!

The enemy will always use scripture to twist truth. The attack was on their relationship with God, with each other, and with the dirt. The plants come from the ground, the earth, and what does humankind have authority over? The ground. And what was Adam's body made from? The ground.

Once again, the fall of the first humans was an attack on their relationship with God, each other, and the earth—the source of their food and physical existence.

God doesn't expect us to just eat salad, does He?

We'll discuss specifics in later chapters. But the point is that you and I are tempted, on a daily basis, to accept counterfeits. We substitute unhealthy food for the real thing. We use food to (temporarily) quiet emotions.

And, like it or not, the result is shame and fear. Should we be walking around in fear? Should we be carrying shame?

This is the source of our problem: we listen to the wrong voice.

So, what about the solution? We'll explore this in the next chapter, but first, consider the personal takeaways below.

Digest and Decide

What seems clear to me from this chapter:

_____

_____

_____

_____

_____

One choice I'm willing to make right now:

_____

_____

_____

_____

"Sorry to wake you -
I can't tell if you're sleeping or doing cardio"

Chapter 4

The Solutions

It takes guts to lose your gut. It takes courage to go against the crowd.

But it's worth it.

Several pastors who've become serious about surviving the garden of eatin' have shared their struggle with us. The problem was the doughnuts. And the pizza, and the cookies. Does your church have a "doughnut ministry"? Sounds like an oxymoron to us.

When unhealthy foods become part of a lifestyle, and part of an organization's culture, it's difficult to change. The stories go like this: a pastor becomes aware of the dangers of processed junk food. He cares about the people. He's faced with a decision.

They can keep the cookies and reinforce harmful eating habits at church, or take a stand for the temples— knowing there would be repercussions.

There would be no more junk food at church. Instead, there would be fruit and nuts. Some people actually left the church as a result. Can you imagine? He had to work through the turmoil, but was willing to stand by the decision because it was the right thing to do. The pastor did exactly what Jesus did (symbolically now). He cleared out the temple! (On a side note, it is pretty ironic these poisonous foods are often served in the foyer right *before* people enter the sanctuary.)

So the story goes on with attendance dropping significantly during the next six months, but *thereafter* grew bigger and stronger than ever.

He didn't condemn people but did stand on the belief that God wants us to be healthy—and we can honor God's will in our choices: spiritually, financially, relationally, and with the food we choose.

Many pastors we've spoken to won't make a similar stand because they are overweight, unhealthy, and often diagnosed as diabetic themselves. But mostly it's because of fear.

If you're a leader—in church or business or community—love those you serve by taking a stand for health.

In your own life, take courage and take a stand against the normal American diet. Love yourself, and those around you, enough to make a change.

His will be done

In Matthew chapter 6, verses 9 to 13, Jesus answered his disciples' question about how to pray. There's much to learn in His answer—about prayer and about life.

> "Pray then like this: 'Our Father in heaven, hallowed be your name. Your kingdom come, Your will be done, on earth

50

as it is in heaven. Give us this day our daily bread, and forgive us our debts, as we also have forgiven our debtors. And lead us not into temptation, but deliver us from evil.'"

Let's ponder the request for "*Your* will be done on earth as it is in heaven." Jesus asks the Father, and wants us to ask the Father, for His will do be done on earth. It is God's intent to have his kingdom principles alive in us. Can we also confidently agree that it's God's intent for us to live with the kingdom principles that coincide with the idea of the Garden of Eden?

Should we eat plants? Should we believe in healing? Should we believe in a perfect relationship with God? Should we take authority over this earth? Of course we should.

Now let's go one step further by digging into 2 Chronicles 7:14:

> "If my people who are called by my name humble themselves, and pray and seek my face and turn from their wicked ways, then I will hear from heaven and will forgive their sin and heal their land."

I want to examine the Hebrew words translated as "heal" and "land." We all understand the concept of healing, which is reconciliation and restoration, but what about the word "land"? It's the same Hebrew word that's noted in Genesis—the word describing what Adam's body was made from! The same earth, the same dirt.

Perhaps God is pleading with us to simply humble ourselves and pray, so we can be healed.

Prayer is a conversation that goes two ways. We have one mouth and two ears for a reason. We need to listen twice as much as we speak. We need to seek. And obey all the wisdom that our loving God provides. And when necessary, we need to repent. The word *repent* is not a scary word; it's a word that says, "I made a wrong turn, and I need to go in the right direction." Because the further we go the wrong direction, the more lost we'll be.

We all need to be humble enough to admit we make mistakes. We need help. If we don't admit that, we shut our communication line off with God. Pride comes before a fall. Just like it did in the Garden when Adam and Eve thought, *I can do what I want, so I can eat what I want.*

We continue to *fall* because we think we can do the same things and expect a different result.

Positive for a change

If we find that we've followed something that's erroneous or harmful, we must not beat ourselves up. We don't need to run away from God in shame like Adam and Eve did. We turn around and get back home—back to truth and love.

When we talk about land and we talk about ground, and if we do those things God says clearly, he will heal our land. In this case he's not talking about the ground outside, he's talking about *our* land. Our bodies. That is, you and me.

> "Do you not know that you are God's temple and that God's Spirit dwells in you? If anyone destroys God's temple, God will destroy him. For God's temple is holy, and you are that temple."
>
> (1 Corinthians 3:16–17)

When we talk about the "temple" in this context, we're referring to the physical body. These temples are made of flesh, bones, organs and tissues. Each cell created from dirt. Yet God chose to dwell in us. You and I are walking around in a flesh suit made of dirt that's been crafted by God.

So, we (in the form of our ancestors, Adam and Eve) messed up in the Garden. We paid attention to the wrong voice, we took one bite, we disobeyed. We believed the lie that said, "Maybe there's a better way than God's way." And we found ourselves in a predicament: separation between us and God.

But God had a remedy. Jesus gave his very life, with a public, humiliating death. He not only gave his life; His body was beaten to the point that people didn't recognize Him. He remedied that situation by defeating death, hell, and the grave. He rose again on the third day.

We are to glorify God in our body, because it is now the temple of the Holy Spirit. In other words, let's start listening to God, instead of our stomach.

Craven cravings

The Apostle Paul had some choice words for those who rejected God and scoffed at His wisdom.

> "For many, of whom I have often told you and now tell you even with tears, walk as enemies of the cross of Christ. Their end is destruction, their god is their belly, and they glory in their shame, with minds set on earthly things."
> (Philippians 3:18–19)

Paul was a bold man. As a former condemner of those that followed Christ, He used to violently persecute the church. But he had a radical transformation of the heart, a radical renewal of mind, a radical change in vision—figuratively and literally.

Because of this, I suppose it was pretty simple for Paul to clearly see the world in terms of right and wrong, good and bad, healthy and unhealthy. "Their god is their belly," he pointed out frankly. But it wasn't just food he was talking about.

Paul was referring to being controlled by a fallen, selfish appetite. Certainly food and drink choices are affected by this mindset. But it goes back to the original sin

54

in the Garden. Surrounded by amazing, delicious foods of countless variety, Adam and Eve chose the one item *not* on their shopping list.

I'll do what I want, and eat what I want, when I want.

This is a clear example of our modern-day hedonistic (all about self-pleasure) viewpoint. Be very cautious as this thought process can lead to a false belief about grace—the deception that we can willingly do anything we want, even if it hurts us, and God can fix it.

God always give us the clear choice between life and death. Yet so many want to have a little from each buffet.

Dessert menu

What feels better, five minutes of chocolate cake, or five days of health?

The choice is obvious, yet we pause and consider the options.

This is not about shame. It's not about condemnation. It's not about ridicule. It's about pure love.

We love you, and want to see people walk in health so they can live the lives they were designed for.

It's time to take action.

Digest and Decide

What seems clear to me from this chapter:

_____

_____

_____

_____

_____

One choice I'm willing to make right now:

_____

_____

_____

_____

_____

Everything was fine until the kale arrived...

58

Chapter 5

Living Alive

Bob had always done life a certain way. He was fairly active, but has always been overweight—and his cholesterol has always been out of control, despite a "healthy" dose of medications.

Bottom line: he didn't feel alive.

When he finally came to see us, he was ready for a change, but didn't know what to do. We presented two options and two outcomes: keep going on the current path, or make some bold changes.

He chose to make changes in his thinking and actions. Within a few months, his body composition radically changed, and he was able to stop taking cholesterol medication. His whole world changed, and the effect rippled through his family, friends, and coworkers.

Bob went from the walking dead to the living alive. His story may seem unusual, but trust us, we see this all the time and have come to expect it on a routine basis.

I am the broccoli of life

We've heard people come against our dietary recommendation to avoid bread.

Their response usually points to the Last Supper and, "Jesus didn't say, 'I'm the *broccoli* of life,' He was the *bread* of life."

Funny. And a completely reasonable issue to explore.

From a medical standpoint, the wheat and the kernels that Jesus and His disciples ate were far different than the grains growing in the western world today. The typical wheat kernel has six times more DNA than the human DNA. It has been genetically modified multiple times over during the last forty years to produce sustainability, and to adapt to herbicides—namely RoundUp, which contains a likely carcinogen.

It's "Frankenwheat"—a scary monster made from an unnatural collection of hideous parts.

And what gave rise to these gruesome grains? Like *The Mummy*, they came from a pyramid. Not an Egyptian one, the "Food Pyramid."

You've seen the icon and its dietary recommendations of six to eleven servings of grains—per day! People believed the pyramid. The spike in demand created the "need" for more processed food, and genetically modified organisms (GMOs).

Who can possibly eat that many servings of grains every day without having weight and health issues?

We can trace the rise in obesity and many diseases along the same time that the Food Pyramid was promoted. (They've since modified the design to a "plate," and it reflects fewer grains.) Thirty years ago, the obesity rate in most U.S. states was under ten percent, and now most states are over twenty-five percent, with many over thirty percent. (https://www.stateofobesity.org/adult-obesity/)

By 2030, it's predicted that 50% of the entire country will be obese. This is simply shocking. We have to do something about this.

Something smells fishy

We're often asked, "Do you only advocate a plant-based diet? What about fish?

After the flood (and after eating who-knows what on the ark for forty days) God gave Noah and his family some menu suggestions. In Genesis chapter 9, he introduced meat and fish—to what was clearly the intended diet of plants and seeds. When it comes to meat, we have the same genetic/hormone/antibiotic modifications concern we have with grains. In addition, we now have factory farms, hormones, pesticides, and other concerns about cleanliness.

But fish (wild-caught) are largely unaffected by these issues. And human genetics haven't changed much in six-thousand years, so fish is still an important source of nutrients. There are not enough essential fatty acids in meat, and that is where fish comes in.

Farm-raised fish can have high Omega-6 content, but very low Omega-3 content. Generally speaking, people need more Omega-3s.

When we look through the scriptures, we don't see evidence of ailments like heart disease, diabetes, cancers, or autoimmune, diseases. We see issues with cleanliness (bacterial) or viruses.

Maybe it's time to catch (and eat) some fish.

Time for a helping of encouragement

God does not leave us or forsake us. He is *not* a God who simply tells us how bad we are, nor is the Bible a book that tells us how bad we are. God's words—and actions—speak clearly about how loved we are.

He also tells us the right way to go: *Here's the path that leads to life.* (Warning: there are not many people on this path, and it can be a lonely journey at first. It is worth it to have all your years be quality years. The goal is to live longer with quality instead of die longer with disease.)

We know from 3 John 2, that God's people should walk in health, even as our soul prospers. This was God's intent in the Garden, and since God does not change, this is still his desire for us. He gave us plants and herbs to thrive.

We want to see how many have the courage to take some action—to fight for their life, and for the lives of loved ones. Many say they would die for those they love, but will you *live* for them? Will you be an example? Will you break the cycle of disease and depression? Are you willing to stand in the gap and break a generational curse?

Let's look into Paul's words to the Roman church.

"I appeal to you therefore, brothers, by the mercies of God, to *present your bodies* as a living sacrifice, holy and acceptable to God, which is your spiritual worship. Do not be conformed to this world, but be transformed by the renewal of your mind, that by testing you may discern what is the will of God, what is good and acceptable and perfect."
(Romans 12:1–2, emphasis added)

We're to present our bodies as a living sacrifice. Sounds uncomfortable, doesn't it? I'd prefer to present my body into a comfy recliner. But that's not the way to become healthier—spiritually or physically. We may have inadvertently begun to present our bodies as nearly dead sacrifices.

Another uncomfortable aspect of these verses is the line, "Do not be conformed to this world." One of the reasons so few people fight for optimal wellness is because the pursuit seems so . . . weird—when compared to what's "normal" in our society. We routinely are labeled as *freaks, radicals,* or *health nuts.*

Really? When did it become strange to live healthy? The answer—when Satan deceived us to believe sickness is a normal part of life.

But when you look at our culture and alarming statistics, do you really want to fit in?

63

Weird or well?

In our society, it's weird not to have donuts for breakfast. It isn't "normal" to not add bacon to every meal. Cola and candy are common fuels to power though the day.

There's so much pressure these days to fit in to society, we stop fitting into our clothes. And we stop fitting into the plan God has for us.

As Bible believing people, what if the path to being relevant is being different?

We need to be relevant because we offer hope for healing—in mind *and* body. Remember, relevance is not looking like and being like the world; it is about standing out to bring positive attention to our Savior, who works in us and through us.

Why do we bother to pray if we have no faith and take no action? We are wasting our time going through nothing more than a ritualistic religious experience. But this is not about religion. This is about a *relationship* with God. And our God wants the best for you.

Religion is man's best attempt to reach God, and hence becomes a fatal disease. (Yes, you can quote us on that!)

Be the weird one at the party who eats the carrots and doesn't eat the nachos. And be the well one. It is kind of like ice cream. You have choices: chocolate or vanilla. Which one are you going to choose? With lifestyle, which one will you choose? Will you choose the lifestyle that leads to chronic sickness, or will you take action and choose the path that brings health and vital life?

For us, being labeled "weird" is not unusual. We are called radical, overbearing, non-compromising, and accused of not having any fun. (Isn't it strange how people often equate *food* with *fun?*)

Of course, none of those things is true about us. We're simply not following the herd—and not eating the herd.

Look at photos of people from fifty or sixty years ago. Most people were slim and fit. Today, the opposite is true. Yes, we have amazing technology compared to the twentieth century, but in many ways, we're less healthy as a society.

When our patients follow the program and begin to lose weight, can you guess the most common reaction they hear?

"Are you okay? You look sick."

An older patient recently told us about a visit to her primary care physician. She was asked what medications she took and answered, "None."

The staff did not believe her and questioned her repeatedly. Taking medications is a "normal" way to live, but it's no way to live if you can avoid it. (Do not stop taking prescribed medications unless directed by a physician, of course.) Why would you resign yourself to taking a handful of medications for the rest of your life? There are no true "medication deficiencies" like there are vitamin deficiencies. Why do we accept it as normal?

But we all can avoid foods that hurt us. It's worth it to be weird. What we really need to become are walking billboards of health and hope. Now that is the best form of advertisement!

Standing up to yourself

Let's look at Jesus' words in Luke 9:23:

> "And he said to all, 'If anyone would come after me, let him deny himself and take up his cross daily and follow me.'"

What does it mean to deny yourself? Sounds like sacrifice. Seems painful. Sounds like our will and emotions are not going to enjoy it—in the moment, anyway.

Jesus denied himself and went to the cross; and He asks us to do the same, in our own ways, to honor God. Why? because it's not about us, it's about others.

People need hope. They don't need a bunch of words. They don't need judgment. They don't need condemnation. They need hope. Most of all, they need an example. Will you be an example to others? Will you pick up the health torch and carry it?

What you believe is crucially important. But what you *do and how you live* —on a daily and hourly basis—are the best ways you can help others in your world.

Digest and Decide

What seems clear to me from this chapter:

_____

_____

_____

_____

_____

One choice I'm willing to make right now:

_____

_____

_____

_____

"My class reunion is next week, can we make this quick?"

Chapter 6

Walking a New Path

During their very first visit, we ask our patients to tell us about their hopes and goals.

Where do you see your health?

What do you want to do in life?

What does retirement look like?

In our experience, you have to *see* a clear vision of their future. Most people have a clear view of their past. But that's like driving down the road while only looking in the rearview mirror—it's a great way to crash.

People look at their past failures, where they fell down and made bad decisions, and they crash again because they can't keep their eyes on a hopeful vision.

Looking up

When Jesus called Peter to step out of the boat and walk to Him (on water!) things went amazingly well. At first.

But after a few steps, he stopped looking at Jesus and started looking at the storm. The waves. The impossibilities that made no sense to his brain and past experience as a fisherman.

When we have a clear goal, we can focus on the steps, and focus on the One who wants to help us walk in health.

It really is that simple. The difficult part is not getting in the way of our own progress.

For example, do you say things like, "I'm addicted to sugar," or "I always gain the weight back"?

What has been the result?

May we prescribe some healthy words? Imagine what might change if we made a habit of statements like this:

"I always achieve my goals."

"I make good decisions."

"My body is the temple of the Holy Spirit."

When Peter began to sink into the water, what did he do? He asked for help.

Peter stepped out and did the impossible, based on faith in God's Word. But then he did what we often do—we changed our focus to our own abilities in relation to the "impossible" circumstances.

Stay connected to God on this journey. Make your close, personal relationship with God your natural way to live. Don't let failure or shame keep you away from God like Adam and Eve did.

Ed on the edge

Ed and his wife came to our clinic for a visit last year. He had been a patient of ours and made wonderful progress.

But Ed's bad health habits made the road more difficult for him.

He weighed in at almost 250 pounds. According to him, Ed was in "the worst shape of my life"—mentally, emotionally, spiritually, and physically. Oh, and he hated his job. It's safe to say he was not a lot of fun to be around.

In addition to all these challenges, he had diabetes and heart disease. Ed was teetering on the edge.

After a thorough exam, we said, "Look, man, you need to go *all in* and not compromise. If you do what we tell you to do, with 100% certainty you'll be better."

Ed paused for a moment. The silence was as thick as cholesterol in a plugged-up artery.

"Alright," he grunted. "I'm going to take your word and do exactly what you say."

Fast forward two months, and we were excited for his next appointment. It was December, and we wondered how Ed was handling the holiday-feast pressure. Our hopes were confirmed when we saw him, looking much better than during our previous visit.

The weight of our words

"Ed! You look good. Have you had trouble avoiding all the holiday meals and desserts?"

"No. Because I'm in. I made you a promise, and I kept my word."

Ed kept his word—not just to us and his wife, but to *himself*.

Keeping your word to yourself can be even more transformational than only keeping your word to others. You can't keep your word to someone else until you've learned to keep your word to yourself.

We saw Ed a few weeks ago, and I barely recognized him. He was slim, trim, and muscular.

I checked his statistics on our body composition machine. In just four months, he lost forty-two pounds of fat and gained nine pounds of muscle. His body fat went from thirty-two percent to nineteen percent. He was now one percent away from his goal and feeling better than ever.

Even though we've seen hundreds of success stories like this, the results still thrill us.

Ed also told us about a recent visit to his primary care physician, who even before testing him wanted to put Ed on more diabetes medications. He told the nurse to check his blood work first.

The next day, the nurse called him with shocking news. "I don't know how you did it, I don't know what you've done, but you're not diabetic anymore. You won't need any medications. Keep doing what you're doing." But the only ones who were shocked were Ed's nurse and physician.

I have my life back

Ed turned to us and said, "Let me tell you about my life. From the time I was fourteen and up to age twenty-nine, I was a partying, hell-raising son-of-a-gun (he actually used a slightly different phrase). I was a drinker, I was a partier, I took drugs, I did it all."

"When I was 29, I had an epiphany. I took all the booze and drugs and cigarettes and threw them in the trash. I turned my life around because I wanted to be someone my mom was proud of."

"I haven't had a drink ever since, and that was twenty-five years ago. But this health transformation has been much more rewarding than giving up all the alcohol, the drugs, the cigarettes—because now I have my life back."

He told us he's got his family back, his relationship with his wife was back, and his relationship with himself is back. He goes to work every day—it's still not his favorite job, but he's able to cope. And now he's seeing the positive effects of his new life; people are drawn to him because he's given them hope.

He actually told us it was easier to give up drugs, booze, and cigarettes than it was to give up cookies and comfort food. He further stated the reward of making lifestyle alterations exceeded that of giving up the other things.

That's right, stepping away from sugar is harder than giving up an addiction to crack cocaine. The two substances stimulate the same pleasure center in the brain—an area bathed in a neurotransmitter called dopamine. Eating sugar is more addicting than dope, and it acts like dope on the brain. Sugar in, "dope" on.

When that little happy feeling goes away, a person will seek more sugar (dope). It is a vicious cookie cycle for lack of better terms.

Ed turned his life around—so drastically, in such a short time—by believing in something bigger. His commitment level was so powerful that he didn't let anything get him off track.

Personally, we believe he could have walked on water if he tried. Because he kept his eyes on the goal.

Faith takes action

When you study the healings of Jesus in the Bible, we clearly see God's heart of love and desire for us to be well. And we also see a theme of action or obedience.

The woman with the issue of blood made an effort to push through the crowd. The man with the withered hand was asked to reach out his arm. When Jesus told people to wash, they did—and were healed. We could cite many other examples, but the point is clear.

Faith in action precedes healing.

Let's be clear: the love and goodness of God is the beginning and end of every good thing in life—including health and healing. But often, our actions are in the middle of the equation.

Your action might mean investing money in healthful foods or scheduling a visit to a specialist. It might be investing time in exercise and prayer. You've invested time and money in this book. We hope you'll take action based on what you've learned.

We hope you'll simply move, walk, and exercise a little more today. Take action toward a more whole and healthy you. We know that speaking God's Word is an action that will produce good fruit.

People who take action go from spectators to participants. Let's stop being participants while the world expands the garden of eatin' and the consequential victims.

People who take action go from watching others' transformation to living their own transformation.

Taking the next step is so important. It's like salvation. Jesus took the first step: "I love you. Come to me." We must respond and take the next step. The same is true for any relationship and any transformation.

The next step is surrendering to the call of God because He does want us to be well.

Continual action continues health

Prayer is a constant communication process. Prayer is a conversation with a God who loves you, who's there all the time. He *always* wants that conversation with you.

Abiding prayer doesn't need to be a ritual. Prayer is just understanding that God is here. For example, we could say, "God, thank you for being here with me, I recognize your presence, tell me what you want me to do, show me how to reach my goal, show me the way."

Prayer is constant. Society has made prayer a ceremony when it's simply a reflection of an awe-inspiring relationship.

In the garden, Adam and Eve communed with God on a daily basis. This was not a *ritual*; this was a *relationship*. When they lived in connection with God, they were blessed. When they departed, in the form of disobedience or hiding, they lost the connection and lost the blessing.

Back to the garden

We hope you'll agree with the following statement: God's intention for us has always been—and will always be—life, health, and love.

The garden of Eden was paradise. Adam and Eve didn't strive to earn the blessing of life; it was a gift—a gift of such abundance, they took it for granted.

When this was lost, sacrifice was required to restore some semblance of goodness on the earth.

Since the Fall, the human experience has been filled with goodness and tragedy, grace and repercussions, joy and sadness, hope and disappointment.

But God's dream for us has never changed.

A new path

Yes, the choice is *clear,* but the choice is not *easy.*

It's simple to want health. It takes some work to fight for it.

Look at Jesus words in Matthew 7:13-14:

> "Enter by the narrow gate. For the gate is wide and the way is easy that leads to destruction, and those who enter by it are many. For the gate is narrow and the way is hard that leads to life, and those who find it are few."

Perhaps, in the context of your quest for health, we'd say it this way: "It won't be easy, but it's worth the effort." And there will be effort. It requires daily effort and rightward action.

Clearly, Jesus is talking about the way to heaven. But is His concern for you limited to what happens *after* you leave this world? God wants heaven to be on earth. Kingdom principles, and the fight to live them, are for right here and right now.

This poses an interesting question. Why is it that we do not cheat on our marriage, we don't cheat on our taxes, we don't cheat on our finances or businesses, yet we cheat on our health?

Why would we choose to destroy the only vehicle that we possess to truly get around in? Our bodies are a precious vehicle that requires the best nutrition and care to have the best possible health.

Change is work

Your job is to decide and step—take action on the narrow, "weird" path. It's narrow, it takes courage, and it's a road where few travel. But God will strengthen you when you move.

Be honest. Deep inside, you want to stop drifting downstream. You want to fight. You want life.

You are likely tired of diets, as diets never work. People who go on diets feel like they are going to *die*, just like the first three letters of the word. Then they throw the whole process out and end up far worse for the wear. Another vicious cycle.

We hear the criticism all the time. "Dr. Michele and Mark, you guys are just too radical—a little too strict. You put so much emphasis on the physical body. Loosen up, will ya?"

But guess what? The criticisms don't faze us. We've heard it all. It's worth it when we wake up feeling healthy and strong. It's worth it when we greet a patient who's beginning to experience healing. It's worth it when we pause and thank God for the thousands of lives we've helped transform.

Physical health is part of your spiritual health. Think about it. Do you feel "spiritual" when you have a bad cold?

There's nothing worse than dying through life.

The path to health requires change: renewing your mind, thinking differently, choosing differently, and spending differently—just *being* different.

Yes, it takes time and money to have the oil in your car changed. But your car will carry you much farther and save you money in the long run.

We don't have any idea the length of our life, but we do have control and authority over the quality of our life.

Ponder on that a moment. The key lesson here is to understand what is in your responsibility of control and what is not. We are not robots. God gives us a brain and the ability to use it. Let's strive for the highest quality of life.

Digest and Decide

What seems clear to me from this chapter:

_____

_____

_____

_____

_____

One choice I'm willing to make right now:

_____

_____

_____

_____

_____

Chapter 7

Back to the Garden

What does "paradise," or "heaven on earth" mean to you?

What good hopes and dreams do you have for your life?

We always ask new patients, "What are three areas about your life—or health—that you hate?" and "What are three areas you want to improve?"

If we can *specifically* identify the areas the individual wants to change or improve, that's "paradise" for people. This is not a shallow exercise. After all, we were created for paradise. Certainly, this world is not paradise, but the Kingdom of God has come to begin the process of redemption throughout creation.

God wants your best life. He wants Eden life to permeate *your* life as much as possible. Still skeptical? Read, and ponder, Jesus' words:

> "The thief comes only to steal and kill
> and destroy. I came that they may have life
> and have it abundantly."
> (John 10:10)

If you've just read those words for the first time, we hope you are blown away by the contrast and clarity of God's love. If you have that verse memorized but don't really believe it is true for your life, we hope you'll take a fresh look at the truth.

The thief (Satan) wants to kill your life as your live your life. He doesn't care if you die. He just doesn't want you to exhibit the life of Jesus while you live. Jesus came that you may have life and have it abundantly.

Seeing your garden

Proverbs 29:18 says,

> "Where there is no prophetic vision, the people cast off restraint" and other translations say that when there is no vision, the people perish."

A lady in her forties came to our office for help. She was open to making changes, but something was missing. Hardships of life and poor health had drained her vision. She had no clear hope for the future.

"When's the last time you felt awesome?" we asked. "And do you have any photos of that time?"

She pulled out her phone and scrolled through pictures for several moments. Suddenly her somber face lit up into a bright smile. She had an image of abundant life.

"Tell us what you see."

"I see someone happy, and I see someone healthy." As she paused, her eyes filled with tears. "I see someone with joy."

"That person is *you*. That's who you've always been and who you'll always be. But you have to see that as a present-day reality and not merely a snapshot from the past."

We're thrilled to report that this woman has kept her eyes on the vision. In just the first two months, her health—and life— were transformed in remarkable ways. What's your vision?

Looks can be deceiving

A couple in their fifties came to our clinic. She suspected there were issues with her hormones, and her husband was there for support and to help with the long drive from their home.

As we engaged in friendly conversation, we asked the husband about his health. We learned he was a former champion in a certain sport. And we learned he was in denial with his health issues. (His wife's sobbing confirmed this beyond any doubt.)

He thought that because he was not overweight, he was perfectly healthy. She watched him pummel packages of cookies and bags of chips—drink bottles of wine in just one sitting—and constantly seek more. His junk food appetite was never satisfied.

We know as practitioners, this person could not possibly have healthy blood biomarkers or body composition. His poor health habits were affecting not only his health but his wife's health with the amount that she worried about him.

I (Michele) found myself saying, "You think you're healthy because you *look* good?"

"Uh, yeah."

"You're probably so unhealthy right now you are affecting this lady's health as she worries about you."

The exam room became so quiet we could hear each other's heartbeats.

"Okay, I'll take your blood test," he sighed, "and the other things you want to do. I'll do your body composition analysis."

A few days later, the test results arrived. His body composition indicated that he was sarcopenic obese ("skinny fat"). His biomarkers indicated he was prediabetic, and skating on much thinner ice than he could have imagined with his vascular health. The results were quite a shock to him. But we're happy to say he jumped in to take action, along with his wife.

They both are pillars of health today. They are walking billboards of health and hope for other people.

Even if their health didn't improve, the improvement in their relationship was dramatic. Today, they are a true power couple, an example to their family and friends.

This couple was faced with the reality of poor health made worse by denial and disagreement. They chose a different vision, and by God's grace, they are living it every day.

We still stay in touch, and recently we asked, "What's the greatest thing you learned from this journey?"

"I learned to pray with my wife, and listen to her. Really listen. I learned to put God into our marriage, because that's where the power comes from. I learned that my good health is a symptom of staying connected—to God and to those I love."

Small steps

It's never too late to make a change and enjoy the benefits.

> "If my people who are called by my name *humble themselves*, and pray and seek my face and *turn from their wicked ways*, then I will hear from heaven and will forgive their sin and *heal their land*."
> (2 Chronicles 7:14 emphasis added)

Small steps are big steps. The first step is humility—a change of heart.

The next step is to have a clear vision.

Then take a step toward that vision. When you step forward, God can step forward into your life.

Decide and Declare

Now: Three areas I dislike about my health and life right now:

_____

_____

_____

Vision: Three areas I desire for my life, (and I believe God wants for me):

_____

_____

_____

In the book of Revelation (22:1–2), John describes the new garden and the Tree of Life:

> "Then the angel showed me the river of the water of life, bright as crystal, flowing from the throne of God and of the Lamb through the middle of the street of the city; also, on either side of the river, the tree of life with its twelve kinds of fruit, yielding its fruit each month. The leaves of the tree were for the healing of the nations."

God's will for us is health in every area of life. It has always been His desire, and always will be.

Confession and prayer for wellness

Thank you, Father for showing me, from Your Word, that you are good. You want life and health for me.

I'm sorry that I haven't always believed that. I'm sorry I haven't taken care of myself with Your love and strength in mind.

But I know You are good, merciful, and Your desire for my life never changes.

Help me own a clear vision for better life and health. I thank You that I have Your best design for my health, and that I represent You and Your Kingdom principles with excellence. I am grateful You give me everything I need, in massive abundance, to achieve this.

Strengthen me as I make better choices, step toward the vision, and set new goals.

When I mess up, help me receive your forgiveness and keep moving forward. I will not stay stuck because I am not a failure.

You can work all things for good—even past mistakes and my current circumstances—because I love You, and I want Your will to be done in and through my life. I know my best days are ahead and begin today. Thank you for making my best better each day of my life.

I pray you use my life to inspire others, and help people know how awesome You are.

In Jesus' name. Amen.

Michele Neil-Sherwood, DO & Mark Sherwood, ND

Mark Sherwood, Naturopathic Doctor (ND) and Michele L. Neil-Sherwood, Doctor of Osteopathy (DO), have a full-time wellness-based medical practice in Tulsa, OK, called the *Functional Medical Institute* where they adopt a whole-person approach, which is outcome-based looking at each individual's unique needs. With a huge vision to change the world health care crisis one person at a time, their mission is to lead people down a pathway of true healing. To that end, there are two purposes: 1) To eradicate all self-imposed, choice-driven disease conditions, and 2) To eliminate the usage of unnecessary medications. Through their unique clinic, various diagnostic tests are used, including genetics, bio-impedance, neurotransmitter, vascular aging, and stress management. The couple host a weekly television program airing regionally in the Midwest US. They serve patients in nearly every state in the US and in several countries around the world.

Drs. Mark and Michele coauthored several books, including two Amazon best-sellers, *The Quest for Wellness* and *Fork Your Diet*. They have been seen on national TV, been quoted on CNN, and are regular contributors to many national publications. With a broad social media network that spans the globe, Drs. Mark and Michele's influence is broad, reaching nearly two million people annually. Their newest project, a full-length movie entitled *Fork your Diet – the movie*, was recently released.

Dr. Mark has completed training and certifications in age management, functional medicine, nutrigenetics, nutrigenomics, hormone therapy, stress management, GI health, and immunology. He is a 24-year retired veteran of the Tulsa Police Department, where he logged a decade of courageous service on the department's SWAT Team. He is also a former Oklahoma state and regional bodybuilding champion, and ex-professional baseball player. Dr. Mark's passion for wellness motivated him to develop several wellness-based courses, which he teaches to law enforcement professionals, corporations, and churches throughout U.S. and worldwide. Mark is a licensed minister and motivational speaker whose presentations are sought by audiences nationwide. His passion and experience for total wellness make him a versatile role model for people of all ages.

Dr. Michele is double board certified (internal medicine and sports medicine) and specializes in the following disciplines: Age Management Medicine, Naturopathic and Functional Medicine, Acupuncture, First Line Therapy, Lifestyle Coaching, Prolotherapy, and soft tissue modalities of Osteopathic Manipulative Therapy. She has an extensive fitness and athletic background including Martial Arts (brown belt, Judo; Black belt, Tae-Kwon-Do), Strength Training/Physique (multiple state and national titles), Russian Kettlebell System (RKC Certified, CK-FMS Certified), and Primal Move Certified).

The couple understands the importance of nutrition, medical food & supplementation, exercise prescription, rest, stress management, hormone balance and the functional movement. This makes them a modern day "dynamic duo of wellness."

More Free Resources for Healthy Momentum

Please take time to review your notes at the end of each chapter.

We couldn't possibly pack everything you need for your journey to wellness in one book. So we've created bonus resources for you.

Go to: www.Sherwood.TV to receive our newsletter and unlock special resources and free downloads. See you there!

And remember, there is strength in numbers.

If you found this book inspiring, buy copies for friends, and start a group to discuss and move forward together!

Faith in Action for Wellness

Now that you have a firm faith foundation for health, here are some practical steps and information for the journey.

If you haven't completed the "Digest and Decide" questions at the end of each chapter, please prayerfully complete those *before* you jump into action.

Setting Goals and Making Plans

Just like financial debt, wellness debt didn't accumulate overnight, or even in a month. In the same way, you should realize you'll need patient, sustained changes to improve your wellness.

When setting goals and making plans, you'll need to simultaneously give yourself a break and be lovingly honest with yourself. Give yourself a break and recognize that short-term "fixes" won't work.

Don't try another crash diet or an unrealistic exercise plan.

Be lovingly honest with yourself by not being brutal. Don't beat yourself up, but face the facts. You're worth investing in!

Facing the Facts

We ask patients the question, "Do you believe the foods you normally eat are good for you?" The answer is usually no.

Then we continue, "Okay, we both agree. Do you love yourself? And do you love your family?" And the answer, at least to the second question, is a confident yes.

"Do you give your children ice cream?"

"Yes," they whisper.

"But you just said it wasn't good for you. Why would you want to hurt yourself and your family, even a little bit?"

At that point, people either make the connection or try to steer the conversation toward the nearest exit. People know what is inherently good or bad for them. What most don't understand is why they intentionally sabotage their health.

We all need to come face to face with the truth. When you face the truth, you have an opportunity to make a decision. It's an opportunity to choose freedom.

So the person with an emotional attachment to certain foods—in this example, ice cream—must ask himself or herself, "What would it be like to *not* want ice cream? Can I imagine that? What would it be like to *not* comfort myself with food?"

Do you love yourself enough to stop hurting yourself?

With a clear, Bible-based vision—and God's help—you can put love in action.

Start Simply to Failure-Proof Your Goals

You have to failure-proof your goals, especially in the garden of eatin.' In society, and maybe in your experience, failure is almost expected.

For example, when we're trying to change the food we eat, we may set a goal to eat one serving of fresh vegetables every day. That's not hard. Or an early goal might be to bring two bottles of water to my desk every day and drink them instead of sugary drinks. Simple.

The point is to develop a habit of forward progress and minimal setbacks. Even in the examples above, the amount of joy and satisfaction you'll experience with "small" successes will surprise you.

We've told patients, "In thirty days, you'll be in a different place. Your blood pressure will drop and start to normalize, your excess fatty tissues will begin to shrink, and you'll be using new, smaller belts in your belt loops."

One goal we often suggest to women is, select an outfit they want to wear and hang it in the closet where they can see it. When they are too small for their current wardrobe, they can give their clothes away and make someone's day.

By the way, if you keep clothes that are too big, you're subconsciously setting yourself up to fail. We want you to set yourself up to win!

Establishing goals

- Identify at least one big goal in each area of your life: physical, intellectual, emotional, and spiritual. You must be specific.

- Create "sub-goals" for each of your major goals. These sub-goals are incremental and, in most cases, sequential. Think of them as "baby steps" toward your big goals.

- Put your goals on a timeline. For example, if your physical "big goal" is to lose twenty pounds, break this down into incremental goals of losing four to eight pounds per month for the next three months. This gives you a goal of losing about two pounds a week, which is a good weight-loss pace that most people can maintain.

- Reward yourself for reaching incremental goals, but don't reward yourself with something unhealthy. In other words, don't reward yourself with a big slice of cake for losing two pounds. That is not rewarding at all. It is actually punishing yourself. How silly is that? Equally important—don't beat yourself up emotionally if you fail to reach an incremental goal. Simply readjust your timeline and keep going.

- Focus on who you want to be as much as on what you want to do.

Enjoy Setting and Reaching Your Goals

Recognize that it takes about ninety days for a habit to truly take root. Some say it only takes twenty or thirty days, but that's not realistic in our experience. It's generally much easier to "get back on the wagon" if you stay focused on a ninety-day goal.

Let's be honest. It isn't possible to stay at peak motivation all the time. Sabbath is a crucial ingredient for success. Give yourself a break occasionally. Relax and enjoy the present moment. Spend time having pure fun with people you love.

Increase Energy and Health Symptoms

There are many tired people in the world, but Ron and Patti may have been the least energized couple ever to (slowly) walk into our clinic for an evaluation.

He was sixty-one, and she was sixty years old. They'd been married almost forty years. Ron was a former athlete in high school and college, but he weighed almost 300 pounds. Patti was about 120 pounds overweight.

They had no energy and were drinking caffeine and consuming sugar all day just to keep moving. Even though they crashed at the end of the day, they slept poorly.

By now, you may be able to guess what we told them. "If you guys will trust us, adhere tightly to your personalized plan, and give it some time, you'll get results and feel so much better."

111

This is not about a "diet;" it is about a lifelong, whole-hearted lifestyle change.

When Patti and Ron started the process with us, they were taking blood pressure medications, cholesterol medications, anti-inflammatory medications, sleep medications, and pills for pain and joint dysfunction, and they were gulping down energy drinks by the six-pack.

No wonder they were tired. In addition, their excess weight was draining energy from them twenty-four hours a day.

Every excess pound of fat tissue we carry is the equivalent of *ten* pounds pushing down on our joints. You have to account for gravity's powerful downward force. Would carrying a backpack full of rocks all day make you tired? That's what Ron and Patti were doing. When you think about it, some folks are carrying an extra "person" around all day long. Talk about having a monkey on your back!

After an initial round of testing, they began to work their plan. In thirty days, we saw significant results, and after nine months, Ron weighed 175 pounds, having dropped over one hundred pounds. Patti dropped sixty pounds. Because they focused on overall wellness and not some crash diet, they not only lost weight, their energy levels were off the charts—and the symptoms of unhealthiness either decreased or disappeared.

"I have more energy now than I did in college as an athlete, and I weigh the same as I did then!" Ron cheered.

As you begin to lose the excess fat, you will have more energy. By the way, Ron now has a six-pack for abs (not energy drinks in his front pockets), and his body fat percentage is what it was in his collegiate athlete days.

Prior to their program, Patti had been severely depressed. She walked with her head down and was ashamed of herself. Because they addressed all four facets of their being, they were also healthier intellectually, emotionally, and physically. And because they helped each other on the journey, their marriage relationship went from okay to great.

Now they both walk with their heads held high and attitudes toward life even higher. From fat, fatigued, and almost dead (as they put it) to fit, energized, and ready to conquer every day, they transformed their lives.

They're excited about the future. They aren't just living for the day anymore; they are living with energy and hope.

Don't Exercise

No, that's not a typo. We actually don't want you to dive into an exercise program until you're ready—and until you've established a relationship with a wellness professional. Simply begin to move more. Think of movement as something you can do to celebrate the God's gift of mobility.

You must understand that food is first. Your relationship to food trumps exercise. This does not mean quit exercising if you are already on an exercise program. This is for the individual who is getting started and has not had exercise as a regular part of his or her life. It is not uncommon for the body to go through a detoxification in the first three months and require more rest at first.

Exercise requires energy. If you don't feel good, emotionally or physically, do you think you'll stick with exercise? Be compassionate and understanding, begin listening to your body, and be realistic.

Begin with nutritional changes, and include changes in your emotional and spiritual life. You will begin to feel better. As you do, and as your energy level picks up, start adding some enjoyable exercise to your day.

We will, however, strongly encourage everyone to move more and sit less. Getting a pedometer is ideal to count steps daily, with ten thousand being the goal. Energy cannot be made up; it must come from within. Exercise will eventually become more fun, stress relieving, and energizing.

Don't pretend you have energy—go get some real energy that will last.

Energy Drinks—The Good, Bad, and Concerning

We are often asked about energy drinks, so here's our take. So-called energy drinks are everywhere. Entire sections in convenience stores are dedicated to them. But are they healthful?

First, let's examine their active ingredient: caffeine. Caffeine has differing effects on the nervous, cardiovascular, and metabolic systems, depending on the quantity consumed. The average dose of caffeine (85–250 mg, the equivalent of three small cups of coffee) may result in feelings of alertness. Higher doses (250–500 mg) can result in restlessness, nervousness, and insomnia.

In high doses, caffeine can even cause hyperadrenergic syndrome, resulting in seizures and cardiovascular instability. A recent report, published by the FDA's Center for Food Safety and Applied Nutrition, cited sixteen deaths related to energy drinks. Yes, you read that right: sixteen!

Energy drinks contain substantially more caffeine than conventional cola or soda-type beverages. Many also contain caffeine-containing ingredients such as guarana and kola—or cola—nut. Researchers once believed that the active ingredient of guarana was a chemical specific to the plant called guaranine. But they later discovered that it was just caffeine.

Kola nut, or cola nut, is likely safe for most people when consumed in foods in small amounts. In larger amounts, the caffeine in cola nut can cause insomnia, nervousness, nausea, and increased heart rate and respiration.

Adding these additional ingredients to an already highly concentrated caffeinated beverage can spike the caffeine levels substantially. The sugars and artificial sweeteners are also unhealthful. It is also important to know that caffeine is a toxin, which the body must work very hard to expel. Sugars and artificial sweeteners, as we have discussed, are inflammatory, immunosuppressive, and even disease-causing.

Dependence on these type of energy drinks is detrimental to your physical health and possibly harmful to all areas of your being.

Symptom Relief

Sickness and disease bring symptoms of *dis-ease*. How does a person find relief from symptoms? There are two main ways.

First, there are drugs and physical therapies that help a person deal with severe pain, discomfort, depression, and biomarkers that are out of balance. We're thankful these are available, but they are not the best long-term strategy.

Second, the ultimate solution to relieving symptoms is getting to the root of the problem—and not just the physiological causes. Is there an emotional component? Are there relationship issues in play? Does the patient have a disease, or is he or she living an inflammatory lifestyle?

If an inflammatory lifestyle is at the root (and the vast majority of the time, it is), we get on top of all those symptoms by decreasing all the inflammatory biomarkers through proper nutrition and lifestyle. And we deal with the other factors, including fear, resentment, anger, unforgiveness, disappointment, and shame (FRAUDS) that breed disease.

Symptoms We Want

By moving away from the standard American lifestyle and eradicating inflammatory living—emotionally, physically, spiritually, and intellectually—biomarkers of health and body composition will improve. And now the symptoms can be positive.

We're all familiar with symptoms of disease, but have you ever considered the symptoms of wellness?

Symptoms of wellness can include joy, happiness, a sense of freedom, hope, motivation, increased energy, inspiration, feeling rested, and peace.

These are some symptoms of wellness. You can experience them!

Less Fat and More Muscle

When I (Mark) was growing up, I was not one of the strong guys and certainly not one of the star athletes. I had good coordination and did pretty well in sports, but you wouldn't have known that from watching me walk down the street.

As an only child who didn't seem to fit in with any group, I got picked on. I even remember a big guy named Butch who thought it was funny to flick my ears as he walked by. He was baiting me, of course, but what was I to do?

I spent a lot of time by myself but also remained very nice to everyone—even Butch. Frankly I was ashamed of who I was and ashamed of how I looked. When I was growing up, if you were chunky, even a little bit, you were fat. And that's how I saw myself. I didn't like my looks, hair, body, or even my thoughts about myself.

In high school, many of my teammates had defined muscles, six-pack abs, and big biceps. They could naturally run fast, jump high, and lift a lot of weight. Deep down, I was embarrassed that I wasn't as gifted. (Please understand, a little chunky *back then* would be classified as not overweight at all now. I am just telling you how I felt at the time.)

I carried a deep sense of shame. But this experience now inspires me to try harder and never quit.

I ate anything I wanted—pizzas, sandwiches, and soft drinks. I remember eating half a loaf of bread every day. I didn't know any better. I was a bucket of inflammation before anybody knew what inflammation was. Food provided a comfort, but not the real comfort I was longing for.

In college, our baseball coach tried to keep an eye on our nutrition—a little bit. But I didn't really learn about wellness until I moved to Australia—on the other side of the world. Talk about a culture shock!

As a baseball player, I had nothing to do all until it was time to play ball each night. There was a gym down the street, and one day I decided to check it out. From that day on, I began to ask questions and apply myself to challenging exercise.

I started lifting weights and eating a little bit better. Guess what happened? My body started to respond. Little by little, fat decreased, and muscle increased.

When I came back to my home town in the United States, I didn't know how much I'd changed, but my friends sure did. Yes, I had more muscle and less fat, but the overall experience increased my confidence and self-esteem—little by little.

As a kid, being ten or twenty pounds overweight was "normal" for me. I guess that's why we are now so opposed to "normal" unhealthiness—because we remember how unhappy we felt, and how much shame that unhealthiness piled on our hearts.

We want you to know there is a better way to live. Even if you had a rough beginning, you can turn your life around. You don't have to be especially gifted—or muscular or athletic—to enjoy how you look and feel.

We know how tough it is to change your outward appearance, because it's so tied to your inward concept of yourself. Remember, your mind must lead the way; your body will follow.

Dropping the Heavy Armor

Fat is sometimes worn like a protective armor, shielding us from fear, resentment, anger, unforgiveness, disappointment, and shame.

People go back to the habits they learned as a child when they are under stress. It takes one time to learn something and a thousand times to unlearn it. You may be on a journey to wellness, but when you're stressed, your old habits will show their ugly heads every single time.

The healthier we get, the less time we spend destroying our lives with negative behavior. Once we know better, we are no longer willing to pay the consequences.

When we think about increasing muscle and decreasing fat, it's not just about *physical* muscle. We want you to be strong in your intellect, emotions, and heart, too. We all need to grow and become stronger in those areas because when we're strong, we can lift more and handle more resistance.

At the same time, we need excess fat to go away physically—and intellectually, emotionally, and spiritually. We must remove gluttonous behavior, insatiable thoughts, and lazy carelessness from our entire being and transform our whole lives. Materialism and consumerism are gluttonous and add harmful fat to our lives while starving our hearts and bank accounts.

Instead of feeling weighed down, the goal is to be lean and fit for the full life you were meant to live. Strive to be that thoroughbred in all areas of your life—more muscle and less fat.

Do Both at Once

This process doesn't stop. Patients start getting stronger—muscle tissue goes up, fat tissue goes down—and we tell them this is your goal for the rest of your life: more muscle

120

and less fat. If we maintain that as a goal, we will be in great shape.

Most people we talk with are convinced they need to get the fat off first and then build muscle later. This simply won't work. Apply yourself to doing both at the same time. In the same way, as you know by now, apply yourself to exercising your intellect, emotions, and spiritual life to build strength (muscle) in your whole person.

Often, those living the standard American lifestyle are not receiving the proper nutrition to optimize their genetic capacity to put on muscle. They're in a state of cellular starvation. Simply changing nutrition to take in the proper macronutrients (protein, carbohydrates, and fat) and micronutrients (antioxidants, vitamins, and minerals) will allow the body to build muscle, and burn fat with little or no exercise.

The body doesn't want to use muscle as fuel. That isn't how it was designed. The body wants to use fat as fuel. We want to get to a place where the body is using the fat that's coming in through our food and even burn some extra fat that's on our frame.

Once there is no excess fat on the frame, we always want to give our engines high-quality fuel to enjoy maximum performance and an energetic state of well-being.

Little by Little

A forty-year-old patient of ours was a good athlete and married to a physician. She was training for a big event, eating the standard American diet and feeling terrible. She worked out longer and harder but had stopped making gains.

She was not recovering, was tired all the time, and even found herself reaching for the anti-inflammatory pill bottle. Her body fat was probably twenty-five percent. She looked good on the outside, but after running so much, her baseline inflammatory markers and body composition were on the rise. She was alarmed to discover she was not as healthy on the inside as she had hoped.

We put her on an anti-inflammatory, muscle-building plan and adjusted her workout—actually telling her to work out a little bit *less*. She was overtraining and wasn't getting results. Her poor nutrition would not support her exercise. She tried to exercise more to keep her weight under control, but that was a mistake. Overexercise and poor diet were creating inflammation and making her sick.

In just three months, she felt much better, and her body fat went down to 13 percent. She was lean, happy, and full of energy. Her inflammatory markers returned to normal.

If she had not taken the time to be evaluated, five years down the road she may have been diabetic and faced the onset of heart disease. Yes, that is possible. Excess exercise, chronic inflammation, and hypercortisolism can lead to Type 2 diabetes.

She recently told us, "I may be forty, but I will give anyone a run for their money. I feel unstoppable."

Little changes can create big results.

How Does Nutrition Help Burn Fat?

The calories burned with exercise certainly have some effect on body composition but not nearly as much as people think. The vast majority of your return on investment in regard to positive body composition change lies squarely with your nutritional protocol.

Insulin plays a role in fat storage, thyroid function, stress hormone production, appetite, metabolism of cholesterol and triglycerides, and sleep. Optimizing insulin is the key.

Chronic production of insulin, predominantly occurring because of ingesting too much sugar, induces all cells, including muscle cells, to become insulin resistant. When this occurs, the body begins to actually produce more insulin, mistakenly believing it needs more. Appetite increases, and the sleep cycle become dysfunctional. At this point, weight gain may begin, especially around the middle, progressing to metabolic syndrome and Type 2 diabetes.

We can attribute this to the standard American diet, which is heavy in starches, sugars, grains, breads, and processed foods. Excess blood sugar with nowhere to go begins to get a grip on structural proteins in the body

(AGEs, or advanced glycosylated end products), accelerating the aging process. Controlling insulin is the key.

You can control insulin to a great degree by what you put in your mouth.

Fat-burning and body-composition-optimizing foods:

- non-starchy vegetables
- fruits
- healthy fats (avocados, nuts, and olive and coconut oils)
- organic or farm-raised protein

Fat-Storing Foods (avoid these)

- processed and fried foods
- soda
- sugars and artificial sweeteners
- MSG
- grains and breads
- corn
- soy

You were designed for health

Physically, your body was designed to be healthy, so it *wants* to get healthy. Give it the food and movement it craves and, little by little, you'll see improvement.

Intellectually, do you believe you can change how your body looks? You can. But you must first change how you look at your body. You might be hiding beneath an armor of excess fat, but the true you wants to emerge and enjoy life. Uncover the superhero inside you. You don't need a phone booth to change; you need to execute your plan.

Emotionally, when you read this chapter, what FRAUDS (fear, resentment, anger, unforgiveness, disappointment, and shame) did you feel? Are you willing to face these and become stronger? Have the courage to face them and overcome. This will build the emotional "muscle" you need to overcome the difficulties of life that try to throw you off course.

Spiritually, what can you do to care for your heart—to help your emotions and willpower? Consider listing affirmations that you can speak out loud daily. Here are a few:

1. I am always free of chronic stress and living a peaceful life.
2. I am in the process of removing excess fat and building more muscle.
3. I am successful in all my endeavors and make routine, high-quality decisions.

The One Thing Holding You Back

You become what you think and speak. If you are not careful, your mind can become a place where negativity and derogatory thoughts reside. It can make your mere existence a miserable experience.

Day after day, year after year, you become what you think and speak. If most of the words that come out of your mouth have a negative tone to them, your life will move toward that negativity. Changing the process starts with evaluating your thoughts and how you speak. Every time you notice a negative thought, evaluate it and turn it around.

For example, if you normally think or say, "I am fat," change those words to "I am being weighed down with a coat of fat, but I am moving rapidly toward healthy body composition and optimum wellness." Speak this positive truth out loud, and invite your body, intellect, emotions, and spirit to the party.

The simple change in attitude and action will help you get you to the gym and help you make better choices at mealtime.

We all want to experience a full, joyful life, right? Well, it doesn't start with running a marathon. It starts with a simple positive thought replacing a negative one. Every journey is one step at a time. Make the next step you take firm, positive, constructive, and uplifting. If you follow this simple walking lesson, you will make huge strides in life.

Face the FRAUDS

We all deal with FRAUDS—fear, resentment, anger, unforgiveness, disappointment, and shame. Part of caring for and guarding our hearts is facing these frauds.

Reducing harmful cholesterol is good, but why stop there? Enjoy a better life by improving your relationship—with yourself, with God, and with those you love.

Endless Servings

Will you speak the following words out loud? It's a great first step.

"I was designed to live in four-part harmony—physically, intellectually, emotionally, and spiritually. My creator loves me, and I will love myself by taking care of all four facets of my being."

Say it one more time, please.

Welcome to your new beginning. Please don't think of this book as "finished." Keep it around as a reference and a reminder of hope.

And please don't take this journey alone. Find a wellness professional who agrees with the principles of this book (or contact us). Find a friend and an accountability partner to help you uphold your health goals.

And ask God for help and guidance along the way. He loves you and wants the best for every part of your life.

We love you, too.

Mark and Michele

⨘: FUNCTIONAL MEDICAL INSTITUTE

We founded the Functional Medical Institute to focus on complete healing, not disease management.

Our doctors and staff are dedicated to helping you stay healthy. We provide the knowledge, resources, and tools to give you a greater understanding of your health.

What is functional medicine?

Functional Medicine is a science-based medical practice that is patient-centered, not disease-centered. We incorporate the best diagnostic tools and technologies from conventional medicine as well as emerging tests and tools to address the underlying root of the illness or disease.

We will help people all over the world:

- Gain muscle and optimize retention well into later years
- Lose fat and become a fat-burning engine
- Balance hormones using the latest in hormone therapy treatments
- Recover from and prevent injuries using PRP and Prolotherapy

- Discover your genetic blueprint, which holds the key to nutritional, supplemental, and exercise prescriptions
- Develop a new relationship with food and food choices
- Regain and retain optimum health and highest quality of life
- We spend time with our patients, get to know their story, understand their specific needs, and create a path for long-term health.
- Contact us at the Functional Medical Institute www.fmidr.com

Does your body feel disconnected from your mind and heart?

There are communication pathways within your body, and when they are disrupted they impact areas like:

- Fatigue
- Anxiety
- Memory loss
- Depression
- Hot flashes
- Headaches
- Reduced sex drive
- Food cravings
- Loss of muscle tissue
- Weight gain

What is this communication system? Your hormones! There are so many myths about hormones, and so many proven ways to get your system back in balance.

Learn more about our video course on this topic at Sherwood.TV

Hormonal balance gives you the ability to be present, every day, in every area of your life.

Invite Drs. Michele and Mark to speak at your event!

Mark and Michele bring hope and health to audiences around the world, with personal stories of transformation and insights gleaned from years of helping people find freedom in every area of life.

Go to Sherwood.TV to learn more

Subscribe to the
Hope and Health podcast.

Founders of a successful medical practice, Drs. Mark and Michele Sherwood bring clear, scientifically-informed ways for you to live a richer life: physically, emotionally, intellectually, spiritually, and financially.

They help people from around the world find the hope and health they were created to enjoy, with simple, actionable insights to help you see results.

Listen and subscribe at www.Sherwood.TV

Made in United States
North Haven, CT
25 April 2022

18558648R00080